Editor
Emily R. Smith, M.A. Ed.

Editorial Manager
Elizabeth Morris, Ph.D.

Editor-in-Chief
Sharon Coan, M.S. Ed.

Illustrator
Nicole Peyer

Cover Design
Jeff Sutherland

Cover Artist
José Tapia

Photo Credit
Digital Imagery © copyright 2000 Corel, Inc.

Art Coordinator
Denice Adorno

Imaging
Ralph Olmedo, Jr.

Product Manager
Phil Garcia

Published in partnership with
Ready Ed Publications
11/17 Foley Street
Balcatta WA 6021
Australia
www.readyed.com.au

Publishers
Rachelle Cracchiolo, M.S. Ed.
Mary Dupuy Smith, M.S. Ed.

Internet Quests

CULTURES OF THE WORLD

Intermediate

Authors

Kellie Lloyd and Jane Bourke

Teacher Created Materials, Inc.
6421 Industry Way
Westminster, CA 92683
www.teachercreated.com

ISBN-0-7439-3410-5

©2001 Teacher Created Materials, Inc.

Made in U.S.A.

Table of Contents

Introduction

How to Use This Book

1. Internet Activity Pages

Note: As this is not an introductory book on using the Internet, you will need to have some understanding of how to navigate the World Wide Web and how to open various Internet addresses prior to attempting these Internet-related activities.

To make use of the pages headed **Internet Activity Pages**, access the *Teacher Created Materials* World Wide Web site at the following address:

http://www.teachercreated.com/books/3410

(Bookmark this site for easy access later.)

When the page opens in your browser, you will see a listing of page numbers and links to Web site addresses. If you click on one of the provided links, you will be taken to the Web page without having to laboriously type the address.

The CD-ROM included with this book also contains hyperlinks that will automatically connect you to the Web sites on the Internet.

2. Alternet Activity Pages

To make use of the pages headed **Alternet Activity Pages**, insert the Alternet CD into your computer's CD-ROM drive. The HTML files on the Alternet CD-ROM require either *Microsoft Internet Explorer* or *Netscape Navigator* to run, so you will need to access one or the other of these browsers. The CD-ROM contains the Alternet package relevant to this book.

The minimum hardware requirement for use of the Alternet program is any computer that uses a frame-capable browser. This includes both Macintosh® and Windows® operating systems.

3. How to Use the Alternet Program

The Alternet CD can be used on Windows or Macintosh systems. Although you will need a browser to view the files, the computer does not need to be connected to the Internet, as all files are self-contained.

You may use the files directly from the CD by clicking on the *Cultures* folder and then opening the file called [*begin.htm*]. For faster operation you can copy the contents of the *Cultures* folder to a folder on your hard disk, remove the CD for safekeeping, then open [*begin.htm*] on your hard disk.

It is recommended that you create a new folder for the Alternet set from each book you have purchased (*Plants*, *Animals*, etc.). Name the folder after the book you are using.

Note: When you load the Alternet program for your students to use, the browser may give warning messages about connection difficulties. This is because you are not attempting to connect to the Internet. You can ignore this by clicking OK.

Note: Purchase of a single book gives you the right to copy the Alternet program on up to 10 computers.

Teachers' Notes

Teacher Information

This series is designed to provide teachers of intermediate children with a multimedia-based set of resources for the Cultures theme.

In using this multimedia resource, students will be required to learn and utilize a range of associated skills such as:

- reading and interpreting given information.
- summarizing given information.
- using generalizations based on given information.
- navigating their way around a Web site.

What does this multimedia approach consist of?

This series aims to provide teachers with a three-pronged approach to meeting the requirements of concepts related to scientific research curriculum. It combines the use of traditional information sources such as reference books and materials with the enormous information capabilities of the Internet and the appeal of computer databases as provided by our Alternet program. As many schools face practical limitations in trying to make use of information accessed through the Internet and computer software, the materials provided here are aimed at having the class working as three groups, each using different methods of information retrieval, which eases the pressures on the available hardware and facilities.

1. The Internet

The use of the related activity pages in this book (titled **Internet Activity Pages**), together with the information sources provided by the World Wide Web, lends a contemporary and exciting aspect to studies in this subject area. As detailed on page 3 of this book, students access the relevant Web pages through the *Teacher Created Materials* Web site and use the information they find to complete the associated tasks on the activity pages.

2. The Alternet Program

The Alternet is a database of information and pictures related to the strand of study on which students are working. Its appearance emulates Web sites found on the Internet's World Wide Web and it is navigated in exactly the same way as the Web through the use of browsers. As with the Internet activities described above, students use the information gathered from the files to complete the relevant activity pages in this book (titled **Alternet Activity Pages**).

3. General Activities

For the activity pages in these sections (titled **General Activity Pages**), students utilize traditional print-related reference materials to complete the tasks on the sheets. It would be useful for a collection of appropriate books to be assembled before commencing the unit so these can be accessed and used with as little disruption as possible. Alternatively, Web site references have been included where possible to provide background information for teachers.

Teachers' Notes *(cont.)*

Updating and Checking of Internet Addresses

The dynamic nature of the Internet means that some sites may change URLs or even disappear altogether. An ongoing role of the publishers will be to monitor changes and post them on our Web site. All addresses used are checked weekly and changes will be posted on our Web site: **http://www.teachercreated.com/books/3410**.

Suggested Use of This Series

As indicated, a multimedia approach has been utilized not only to provide students with a range of reference sources but also to take account of the difficulties schools have in trying to match limited resource access with the requirements of the curriculum. To help teachers plan for these contingencies, this book has been structured to allow units of work where groups rotate from one information source to the next on a week-to-week basis.

It is important to note that the activities in each section are "stand-alone," meaning that students will not need to complete previous activities in order to work successfully. Exactly how teachers choose to use the materials is obviously dependent on the amount of computer hardware and Internet access available, but with a bare minimum in mind, books have been designed to allow a rotation (assuming one period per week is spent on the unit).

To help follow a planning pattern such as this, the following checklist can be used to check off the activity sheets that each group has completed:

1. Where possible, units are evenly balanced as in the cxample below, i.e., there is an equivalent number of Internet, Alternet, and print research activities in each section of the book to allow for easy rotation of groups.

2. Activity pages are designed to take about 25–30 minutes—the approximate length of time usually available in a school period after preliminaries have been sorted out.

Check List

Internet	1	2	3
Earth's Greatest Features			
Languages Around the World			
National Flags			
Festivals and Traditions			
Christmas Around the World			
World Tour			
Travel to Brazil			
Journey to Japan			
A Visit to Ireland			
The Gift of the Nile			

Alternet	1	2	3
The Island Continent			
The United Kingdom			
Land of Ice and Fire			
The Largest Country			
The Kingdom of Nepal			
Saudi Arabia			
Land of Smiles			
¡Hola Amigos!			
Greece			
Jambo!			

General	1	2	3
Countries Around the World			
Climate			
Happy New Year!			
G'day Mate			
Wave That Flag			
Governments			
Multicultural Communities			
Pen Pal			
Travel Brochure			
Bon Voyage!			
Reflection Page			

The World Around Us

Content Area(s):

- geography
- languages
- social studies
- technology

Objectives:

In this section students:
- navigate Web sites and find required information.
- identify major earth features.
- translate English sentences into other languages.
- draw national flags for various countries.
- design a personal flag and identify the symbolism of that flag.

Materials Required:

- computer with Internet access
- pencil or pen

Web Site(s):

- Students need to access the TCM Web page for the Cultures book at:

http://www.teachercreated.com/books/3410

- Students then click on the link to the page on which they are working.
- Allow the children time to familiarize themselves with the Web site before starting the activity sheets.

Time:

- Approximately 30 minutes per lesson

Teaching Tips and Suggestions:

Earth's Greatest Features (page 7)

- Let students know that as they click on the buttons under the map, the information will come up on a chart above or beside the map. If they click on the chart, an "x" will show up on the map to indicate where the feature is located.

Languages Around the World (page 8)

- After students type in the sentence to be translated, there is a button under the text box that allows them to choose what language to translate to.
- It might be fun to make a class dictionary of how to say "hello," or some other common phrase, in as many languages as the class can find.
- It may be interesting to have some students do a report on languages that use a different alphabet than Westerners.

National Flags (page 9)

- This lesson might be introduced with a study of the history of the United States flag.

Name_____

Earth's Greatest Features

Go to **http://www.teachercreated.com/books/3410**

Click on **Page 7**, **Site 1**

- Ever wonder what the name of the world's tallest mountain is or where the biggest waterfall is? Explore the Web site to find the answers.

  1. Which is the largest continent? _____

  2. List the five largest oceans and seas in order from largest to smallest.

     ➤ _____

     ➤ _____

     ➤ _____

     ➤ _____

     ➤ _____

  3. What are the names of the world's two tallest mountains?

     _____

  4. Name the world's three longest rivers and where they are located.

     _____

     _____

  5. Name two volcanoes located in Hawaii. _____

     _____

  6. Which country has four of the world's tallest waterfalls? _____

  7. In which country will you find a lake called Baykal? _____

  8. What is the name of the tallest mountain in North America? _____

- Using the Web site, make up five questions to ask a friend. Write your questions below and the answers on another sheet of paper. Once you have written your questions, switch papers with a friend.

     ➤ _____

     ➤ _____

     ➤ _____

     ➤ _____

     ➤ _____

> **Challenge:** Look at the picture of the world on this Web site.
> Why do you think Earth is sometimes called the "blue planet"?

Name:_____

Languages Around the World

Go to **http://www.teachercreated.com/books/3410**

Click on **Page 8**, **Site 1**

This site translates your words into a number of languages at the click of a button.

❂ Use the Web site to translate the sentences below into the different languages next to each sentence. Use the back of the page if you need more room.

1. What is your name?   In French: _____

   In Italian: _____

2. Where do you live?   In Italian: _____

   In Portuguese: _____

3. Do you speak English?   In Spanish: _____

   In German: _____

4. I am using the Internet.   In Spanish: _____

   In German: _____

❂ Write three of your own sentences and translate them into any languages you want. Be sure to write down which languages you are translating them to!

English:_____

_____:_____

English:_____

_____:_____

English: _____

_____: _____

Egyptian Hieroglyphics

The Ancient Egyptians wrote using picture symbols known as hieroglyphics. See what your name looks like in hieroglyphics by clicking on **Page 8**, **Site 2** and typing in your name.

❂ Draw your name in hieroglyphics in the box below.

Name_____

National Flags

Go to **http://www.teachercreated.com/books/3410**
Click on **Page 9**, **Site 1**

Every country has a national flag that is used to represent the country. Most flags have a special meaning for the country. For example, the Japanese flag shows the red sun, and the Australian and New Zealand flags show the Southern Cross that is viewed only in the southern skies.

✺ Draw the national flag for each of the countries below.

Mexico

Austria

France

Brazil

✺ Design a flag for yourself in the box. On the lines, explain the meaning of your flag.

Challenge: Visit **Page 9**, **Site 2** to play "Where is That?"

Traditions Around the World

Content Area(s):

- language
- social studies
- technology

Objectives:

In this section students:
- navigate their way around Web sites and find required information.
- research the festivals and traditions of a country.
- summarize information.
- contrast their experiences to others' experiences.
- find out how to say "Merry Christmas" in different languages.

Materials Required:

- computer with Internet access
- pencil or pen

Web Site(s):

- Students need to access the TCM Web page for the Cultures book at:

http://www.teachercreated.com/books/3410

- Students then click on the link to the page on which they are working.
- Allow the children time to familiarize themselves with the Web site before starting the activity sheets.

Time:

- Approximately 30 minutes per lesson

Teaching Tips and Suggestions:

Festivals and Traditions (page 11)

- Have a class discussion about how students celebrate different holidays.
- Brainstorm a list of special occasions and holidays. (Make sure that students understand the word *occasion.*)
- Choose a few unusual occasions or celebrations to have in the class. Assign students to find and make food or art associated with the celebrations.

Christmas Around the World (page 12)

- This page does not have to be used during the Christmas season.
- Make sure that students know who the Maori people are (native New Zealanders).
- Emphasize the *Challenge* information. Include any other celebrations or holidays that may pertain to students in your class. This information can be great for comparison and discussion to help students better appreciate similarities and differences in beliefs.

Name_____

Festivals and Traditions

Go to **http://www.teachercreated.com/books/3410**

Click on **Page 11**, **Site 1**

Visit the Web site to learn all about how festivals and traditions are celebrated in different countries in Europe.

❀ Choose a country to study and describe two special events that the people there celebrate.

Name of country: _____

1. Occasion (e.g. birthday, wedding, national holiday): _____
   Describe what happens on this day.

   _____

   _____

   _____

   _____

   _____

2. Another occasion:_____
   Describe what happens on this day.

   _____

   _____

   _____

   _____

   _____

3. What do you do differently to celebrate similar days or holidays?

   _____

   _____

   _____

   _____

   _____

> **Challenge:** Find out more about different countries by visiting the Atlapedia at **Page 11**, **Site 2**.

Name:_____

Christmas Around the World

Go to **http://www.teachercreated.com/books/3410**
Click on **Page 12**, **Site 1**
Christmas is celebrated all over the world in different
ways. Read about how this holiday is celebrated in
other countries by clicking on **Christmas** at the Web
site.

❂ Read the information carefully. Choose a country
and use the space below to describe how
Christmas is celebrated there.

_____

_____

_____

_____

_____

❂ Choose another country to read about. How do the people of that country celebrate
Christmas?

_____

_____

_____

_____

❂ Search around **Page 12**, **Site 2** and find out how to say "Merry Christmas and Happy
New Year" in:

French: _____

Spanish: _____

Irish: _____

Japanese: _____

Challenge: Not all people celebrate Christmas. Do you know of any other holidays
that are celebrated in December? Search the Internet for more information on
Ramadan, Kwanzaa, or Hanukkah. Record what you find on the back of this page.

Traveling the Globe

Content Area(s):

- geography
- social studies
- technology

Objectives:

In this section students:
- navigate their way around Web sites and find required information.
- identify the location and details about various countries.
- draw national flags for various countries.
- find information from a map.

Materials Required:

- computer with Internet access
- pencil or pen

Web Site(s):

- Students need to access the TCM Web page for the Cultures book at:

http://www.teachercreated.com/books/3410

- Students then click on the link to the page on which they are working.
- Allow the children time to familiarize themselves with the Web site before starting the activity sheets.

Time:

- Approximately 30 minutes per lesson

Teaching Tips and Suggestions:

- Have students identify each country that they study on the Countries Around the World Map (page 34).

World Tour (page 14)

- Students click on the countries and cities on the tour guide for more information.

Travel to Brazil (page 15)

- Encourage students to do the *Challenge* activity. This is a wonderful site with plenty of photos.

Journey to Japan (page 16)

- To find the translations for the words in question 9, students will need to pay attention to the blinking box at the bottom of the page.

A Visit to Ireland (page 17)

- Explore with students the aspects of the United States culture that were brought by Irish settlers.

The Gift of the Nile (page 18)

- The buttons on the side of the page will take students to interesting links.

Name _____

World Tour

Go to **http://www.teachercreated.com/books/3410**
Click on **Page 14**, **Site 1**
This site allows you to visit 30 different cities all over the world. Pay attention to which tour you need to click on to find each city below. Enjoy your travels!

○ **Tour 1—Indonesia**

1. How many islands make up Indonesia? _____

2. These islands spread _____ miles east to west across the _____.

3. Which countries does Indonesia border by land and sea? _____

   _____

   _____

4. How many people live in Indonesia? _____

5. What food is used in almost all meals in Indonesia? _____

○ **Tour 2—Mauritius**

6. Mauritian culture is a blend of _____, _____, _____,
   _____, and _____ people.

7. Where is Mauritius located? _____

   _____

8. What did Mark Twain write about Mauritius?

   _____

   _____

   _____

○ Draw and color the flag of Mauritius

○ **Choose a Place**

9. Choose any place on this site that you would like to visit. Write at least four things that you learn on your tour.

   _____

   _____

   _____

   _____

Name_____

Travel to Brazil

Go to **http://www.teachercreated.com/books/3410**
Click on **Page 15, Site 1**
Take a trip to Brazil and discover some of the facts
about this beautiful South American country.

⚙ Complete the sentences below by filling in the
   correct word(s).

1. Brazil is the world's _____
   biggest country in area.

2. It has a population of over _____
   people.

3. The official language of Brazil is _____.

4. A popular Brazilian dance is the _____.

5. Almost one quarter of the world's _____ is grown in Brazil.

6. The _____ rain forest in Brazil contains about 50,000
   species of wildlife.

7. Five native plants found in Brazil are _____, _____,
   _____, _____, and _____.

8. Brazil has more _____ than anywhere else in the world.

9. If you lived in Brazil, you would probably get your electricity
   from _____.

10. The Amazon river is the _____ longest river in the world.

⚙ Draw the flag of Brazil in this box.

Challenge: Take a journey with the children of the Amazon at **Page 15, Site 2**.

Name:_____

Journey to Japan

Go to **http://www.teachercreated.com/books/3410**

Click on **Page 16**, **Site 1**

☼ Zoom over to Japan by visiting this Web site. Learn about the people and culture of this country and complete the questions below.

1. Name the four islands of Japan.

_____   _____

_____   _____

2. How many people live in Japan?_____

3. What sort of foods do people eat in Japan? _____

_____

4. Draw the flag of Japan in this box.

5. What does the flag symbolize?

_____

_____

_____

6. What sort of products do we get from Japan? _____

_____

_____

7. Draw a picture of a Japanese tower in this box.

8. What is the title of the first novel ever written?

_____

9. What do these Japanese words mean in English?

Sumimasen: _____

Arigato: _____

Konnichi wa: _____

Name_____

A Visit to Ireland

Go to **http://www.teachercreated.com/books/3410**

Click on **Page 17**, **Site 1**

☘ Visit the Emerald Isle and learn all about Ireland at the site. Complete the questions below.

1. How many people live in Ireland? _____

2. According to the Web site, why does Ireland look so green?

   _____

   _____

   _____

   _____

3. What languages do they speak in Ireland? _____

4. What might you eat if you visited Ireland? _____

5. What is the capital city of Ireland? _____

6. Sometimes people call Ireland by another name. What is this name?

   _____

7. What holiday is one of the best days of the year in Ireland?

   _____

8. Write three interesting facts about Ireland.

   • _____

   • _____

   • _____

☘ Draw the flag of Ireland in this box.

Name _____

The Gift of the Nile

Go to **http://www.teachercreated.com/books/3410**

Click on **Page 18**, **Site 1**

- Journey to the interesting land of Egypt. Complete the questions below.

  1. Where is Egypt located? _____

  2. How far back does Egyptian culture date? _____

  3. Name three things that the ancient Egyptians first developed:

     _____, _____, and _____.

  4. What is the major religion of Egypt? _____

  5. What is the traditional dress for men in Egypt called? _____

  6. What landform covers most of Egypt? _____

  7. Why is Egypt sometimes called the "Gift of the Nile"? _____

     _____

  8. What percent of Egypt's population lives near the Nile River? _____

  9. What are Egyptian farmers called? _____

- Click on the **Photos** button and complete the activities below:

  10. What is Luxor? _____

  11. What is ancient Egyptian writing called? _____

  12. The Great Sphinx is about _____ feet high and _____ feet long.

  13. Name some types of transportation the people in Egypt use today:

      _____

      _____

  14. What did they use for transportation in the past? _____

- Click on the **Map and Facts** button:

  15. What two seas border Egypt? _____ and _____

Islands or Countries?

Content Area(s):

- language
- social studies
- technology

Objectives:

In this section students:

- navigate their way around Alternet sites and find required information.
- research different English-speaking cultures.
- summarize information.
- compare their culture with other cultures.

Materials Required:

- computer with Internet browser
- Alternet CD-ROM
- pencil or pen

Alternet:

- To use the Alternet CD-ROM, open [*begin.htm*]. For more instructions, see the section titled *How to Use the Alternet Program* on page 3.
- To go to individual pages, students access the index page and then click on the number of the page they are using.

Time:

- Approximately 30 minutes per lesson

Teaching Tips and Suggestions:

The Island Continent (page 20)

- Make sure that students know what a continent is.
- Australia and many other countries of the world are part of the Commonwealth of Countries. Have students research to find out more about the Commonwealth.

The United Kingdom (page 21)

- We often look at England in history books, but very few students understand the role of England and the United Kingdom in our world today. Now is a good time to expand the perspective of this country and look at the changing roles of countries all over the world.
- Watch an English soap opera or other show in class and discuss the differences in language and in humor.
- Have students identify all of the English speaking countries of the world and look for similarities in cultures.

Name _____

The Island Continent

For this activity you will need the **Cultures Alternet CD-ROM**.
Click on the link to **Page 20**.

Land and Climate

1. Why is Australia called the island continent?

   _____

2. What is the middle of this country known as?

   _____

3. What season is it when Australians celebrate Christmas?

   _____

Animals

4. What is a marsupial? _____

   _____

5. According to legend, how did the kangaroo get its name? _____

   _____

   _____

   _____

6. What is the largest kingfisher in the world? _____

The People

7. Who were the first people in Australia? _____

8. When did these people begin living in Australia? _____

9. Name at least three things that are different in Australia today compared to the United
   States. _____

   _____

Fun and Sports

10. What are two different sports that
    Australians play?

    _____   _____

> **Challenge:** Cricket is a very popular sport in many places around the world.
> Research the rules and equipment for the game of cricket. Get some friends together
> and play a game of cricket!

Name_____

The United Kingdom

For this activity you will need the **Cultures Alternet CD-ROM**.
Click on the link to **Page 21**.

Land and Climate

1. Label the four areas of the United Kingdom on the map.

2. What is the nation's official name? _____

3. What are four other names people call this country?

   _____   _____

   _____   _____

Circle **True** or **False** about the statements below:

4. Wales is famous for its rolling plains.   **True**   **False**
5. The United Kingdom has a Mediterranean climate.   **True**   **False**
6. The Gulf Stream keeps the weather from getting too cold.   **True**   **False**
7. The land of the United Kingdom is all the same.   **True**   **False**

History

8. Why are parts of British culture now parts of cultures all over the globe?

   _____

   _____

Food

9. What is the traditional Sunday meal in the United Kingdom? _____

10. Does your family have a traditional Sunday meal? What is it? _____

   _____

Fun and Sports

11. What is one of the most famous sporting events in the United Kingdom?

   _____

12. Scotland is the home of what sport? _____

Fast Facts

13. What is money in the United Kingdom called?

   _____

14. What is a nickname for the flag of the United Kingdom?

   _____

The Great North

Content Area(s):

- reading and comprehension
- social studies
- technology

Objectives:

In this section students:

- navigate their way around Alternet sites and find required information.
- explore the history and cultures of Iceland and Russia.
- summarize information.

Materials Required:

- computer with Internet browser
- Alternet CD-ROM
- pencil or pen

Alternet:

- To use the Alternet CD-ROM, open [*begin.htm*]. For more instructions see the section titled *How to Use the Alternet Program* on page 3.
- To go to individual pages, students access the index page and then click on the number of the page they are using.

Time:

- Approximately 30 minutes per lesson

Teaching Tips and Suggestions:

The Land of Ice and Fire (page 23)

- This could be a good time to discuss geological processes with students. Iceland is at the northern part of the Mid-Atlantic drift and is a very geologically active area.
- Have students research how geothermal water is used for heating houses.
- Students might research the Vikings and create a display or history chart for Viking exploration and impact on the world.

The Largest Country (page 24)

- Until fairly recently, Russia was considered the greatest threat to the United States. Have discussions to assess student perceptions of Russia.
- Study the history of Russia and the United States.
- View part of a Russian ballet or read Russian children's books.

Name_____

Land of Ice and Fire

For this activity you will need the **Cultures Alternet CD-ROM**.
Click on the link to **Page 23**.

Land and Climate

1. Why is Iceland sometimes called the "Land of Ice and Fire"? _____

_____

2. How do Icelanders heat their homes? _____

_____

History

3. Iceland was settled in the late _____ by the_____.

The People

4. How are people from Iceland different from people in the United States?

_____

_____

_____

Recreation

5. What do you think is the reason that Icelanders have the world record for owning books?

_____

_____

Food and Celebration

6. What meat do Icelanders use to make their hot dogs? _____

7. Name the three Viking foods that are still eaten in Iceland today.

a. _____   b. _____

c. _____

Fast Facts

8. What is the capital of Iceland?_____

9. What is Vigdis Finnbogadottir famous for? _____

_____

Challenge: If you were named like people in Iceland, what would your last name be?
Make a family tree on the back of this page and use Icelandic last names for your
family.

Name _____

The Largest Country

For this activity you will need the **Cultures Alternet CD-ROM**.
Click on the link to **Page 24**.

Land and Climate

1. What two continents does Russia stretch across?

   _____

   _____

2. What is one of the coldest regions in the world? _____

3. Because of the cold, only about ___% of the land in Russia can be used for farming.

History

4. Complete the time line about an aspect of Russia's history:

   800s–1922 _____

   1922–1991 _____

   1991–present _____

The People

5. Why do some families in Russia have to share kitchens and bathrooms with their neighbors? _____

Food and Culture

6. Would you like to eat Russian foods? Why or why not?

   _____

7. Where might you go to spend a Saturday afternoon if you were Russian?

   _____

   _____

8. What is caviar? _____

Fun and Sports

☼ Draw a picture of the unique Russian architecture.

9. What do Russians do in the country in the summer?

   _____

   _____

   _____

   _____

Asian Paradise

Content Area(s):

- reading and comprehension
- social studies
- technology

Objectives:

In this section students:

- navigate their way around Alternet sites and find required information.
- draw pictures to illustrate different aspects of Asian cultures.
- summarize information.

Materials Required:

- computer with Internet browser
- Alternet CD-ROM
- pencil or pen

Alternet:

- To use the Alternet CD-ROM, open [*begin.htm*]. For more instructions see the section titled *How to Use the Alternet Program* on page 3.
- To go to individual pages, students access the index page and then click on the number of the page they are using.

Time:

- Approximately 30 minutes per lesson

Teaching Tips and Suggestions:

- These are three very diverse countries that are all part of the Asian continent. You may choose to have students do a comparison/contrast among the three.

The Kingdom of Nepal (page 26)

- The Alternet does not address the problems that some poorer countries face. Encourage students to research or think about how Western influences can pollute poorer countries in need of income (e.g. tourism and Mt. Everest expeditions).

Saudi Arabia (page 27)

- Watch *Lawrence of Arabia*.
- Discuss the very important role that religion has in Arab culture.
- Have students research the gasoline industry and its role in world politics and culture.

Land of Smiles (page 28)

- Play Thai games or have a Thai feast.

Name _____

The Kingdom of Nepal

For this activity you will need the **Cultures Alternet CD-ROM**.
Click on the link to **Page 26**.

Land and Climate

1. Name the three main areas of Nepal.

   _____

   _____

   _____

2. Why is the Himalaya called "The Ceiling of the World"?

   _____

3. What foods are grown in southern Nepal? _____

   _____

History

4. Where is the capital of Nepal? _____

The People

5. What are Sherpas? _____

6. What are Gurkhas? _____

Religion

7. What is the main religion in Nepal? _____

8. In the box below, create a sign of the do's and don'ts to remember when visiting a religious site.

Do	Don't

Celebrations

9. How many festivals do the Nepalese people have? _____

Challenge: On the back of this page, write what you know about climbing to the peak of Mt. Everest.

Name_____

Saudi Arabia

For this activity you will need the **Cultures Alternet CD-ROM**.
Click on the link to **Page 27**.

Land and Climate

1. Saudi Arabia is the world's leading producer of _____

_____.

2. What is the name of the large, sandy desert in Saudi Arabia?

_____

History

3. Why do you think this country was named "Saudi Arabia"?

_____

_____

_____

☉ Read the sections on **People**, **Clothing**, **Way of Life**, and
Food.

4. Write a paragraph about how life in Saudi Arabia is
different from your life on the back of this
paper.

Religion

5. Why do you think this phrase is said, "Islam is more than a religion. It is a way of life"?

_____

_____

_____

Fun and Sports

6. List the different things that males and females do for fun.

boys/men	girls/women

Name _____

Land of Smiles

For this activity you will need the **Cultures Alternet CD-ROM**.

Click on the link to **Page 28**.

Land and Climate

1. What are the three seasons in Thailand? _____

_____

Animals

2. Why have many animals in Thailand become endangered? _____

_____

History

3. What was Thailand called for most of its history? _____

The People

4. What percent of Thai people are Buddhist? _____

5. How can you tell which people are Buddhist monks? _____

Customs

6. What is a "wai"? _____

Homes

7. Draw a picture of what a traditional Thai house might look like. In your picture, include what the area might look like and the type of pet a Thai family might have.

Food

8. Create a menu of foods you might eat in Thailand on the back of this page.

Fun and Sports

9. What American game do you think might have come from the Thai sport "takraw"?

_____

The Warmer Countries

Content Area(s):

- reading and comprehension
- social studies
- technology

Objectives:

In this section students:

- navigate their way around Alternet sites and find required information.
- write an acrostic poem.
- make judgements and justify answers.

Materials Required:

- computer with Internet browser
- Alternet CD-ROM
- pencil or pen

Alternet:

- To use the Alternet CD-ROM, open [*begin.htm*]. For more instructions see the section titled *How to Use the Alternet Program* on page 3.
- To go to individual pages, students access the index page and then click on the number of the page they are using.

Time:

- Approximately 30 minutes per lesson

Teaching Tips and Suggestions:

¡Hola Amigos! (page 30)

- Mexican culture has had a huge impact on the United States. Mexican food, drink, holidays, and language have become part of mainstream American culture. Have students do research on each of these aspects of life to better understand the Mexican culture. Celebrate Cinco de Mayo the Mexican way or have a picnic in a "cemetery" for El Día de los Muertos.
- Mexico also has many exciting ancient cultures to study.

Greece (page 31)

- Incorporate a study of ancient Greece, mythology, and the influence of these on modern cultures.

Jambo! (page 32)

- Review acrostic poems before doing the activity page. You may need to help your students get started.
- Have students create a "safari" play telling about what they find in Kenyan culture.

Name _____

¡Hola Amigos!

For this activity you will need the **Cultures Alternet CD-ROM**.
Click on the link to **Page 30.**

Land and Climate

1. How are the northern and southern parts of the country different? _____

   _____

   _____

   _____

History

2. What is a person that has Indian and Spanish ancestors called? _____

Food and Drink

3. What is the most important food to most Mexican people today? _____

4. Name at least six Mexican foods. _____

   _____

   _____

Clothing

5. Label the picture by writing the Mexican name for each piece of clothing.

Festivals

6. Choose one of the Mexican festivals or holidays.
   Click on it to learn more.

   Holiday: _____

   Describe two things that the Mexican people do to celebrate this holiday.

   • _____

   • _____

Challenge: Read the **Fast Facts** section and draw a picture of the Mexican flag on the back of this paper. Research to find out what it really looks like and compare it to your drawing.

Name_____

Greece

For this activity you will need the **Cultures Alternet CD-ROM**.
Click on the link to **Page 31**.

History

1. What is "Western Civilization"? _____

_____

_____

2. What is the capital of Greece? _____

3. What is mythology? _____

_____

4. Where did the gods and goddesses live? _____

5. Who is Zeus? _____

The People

6. Do you think that a Greek person is like you or very different from you? Explain your answer in complete sentences. _____

_____

_____

Fun and Sports

7. What sporting event did the Greeks hold for the first time thousands of years ago?

_____

8. What sorts of things do Greeks enjoy doing during their free time? _____

_____

_____

Food

9. When do people in Greece usually eat dinner?_____

10. What is a restaurant called in Greece? _____

11. Describe at least three things that Greeks eat that are different from what you eat.

_____

_____

_____

Name _____

Jambo!

For this activity you will need the **Cultures Alternet CD-ROM**.
Click on the link to **Page 32**.

Land and Climate

1. Where do most of the people in Kenya live? Why? _____

_____

Animals

2. What does "safari" mean in the Swahili language? _____

History

3. When did Kenya become an independent nation? _____

The People

4. An acrostic is a poem using the letters of a word as the first letter in a sentence or verse about the word. Write an acrostic about Kenya.

K_____

E_____

N_____

Y_____

A_____

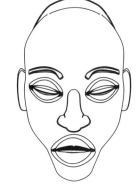

Culture

5. What are three things that Kenyans make or create for their family and friends or for special occasions? _____

_____

Food

6. What is the most important food in Kenya? _____

Fun and Sports

7. What are Kenyans known for in sports? _____

Fast Facts

8. What is the official name of Kenya? _____

9. What is the national language of Kenya? _____

10. What is the money in Kenya called? _____

Fun Facts on Countries

Content Area(s):

- language
- map skills
- social studies
- research

Objectives:

In this section students:

- identify, locate, and use resource materials to find required information.
- identify countries and color code a world map.
- write a story using Australian slang.

Materials Required:

- library, computer, or other resource materials
- pencil or pen

Time:

- Approximately 30 minutes per lesson. These lessons might also be used as part of ongoing research.

Teaching Tips and Suggestions:

Countries Around the World (page 34)

- This page is intended to be used as part of a portfolio or as a record of cultures that are studied. You might opt to use this as a one-time activity by having students color and label 24 countries around the world. Review how to use a color key for the map.

Climate (page 35)

- Establish a world map and separate it into climate zones. Have students draw and paste pictures depicting each area on the map.

Happy New Year! (page 36)

- Celebrate the New Year as other countries do throughout the year.

G'day Mate! (page 37)

- Try to find an Australian to visit the class. Have students share their stories with the class. Watch or listen to an Australian TV or radio program.

Name _____

Countries Around the World

As you learn about countries all over the world, color them in on this map and label the key. Be sure to label the oceans as well.

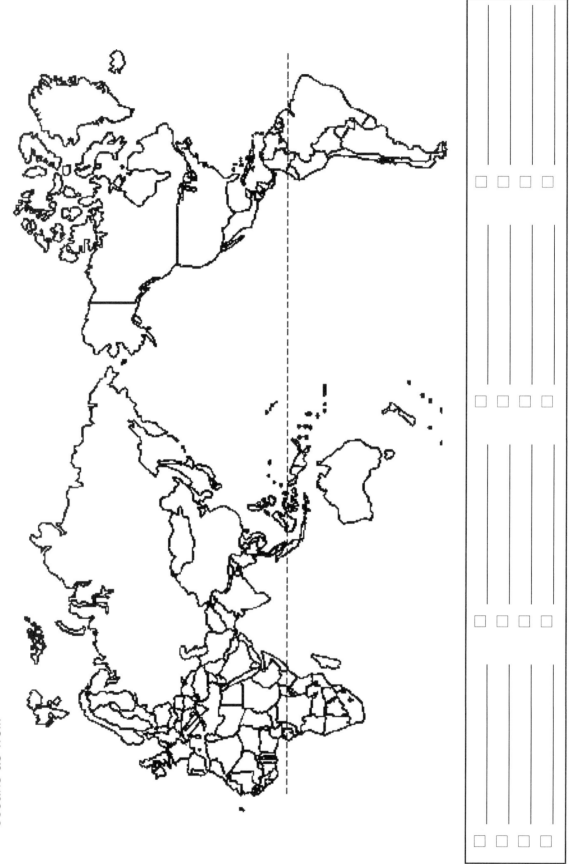

Name_____

Climate

☼ Use your library or other resources to find the information to complete this activity page.

Climate is the usual weather patterns in a particular area. Different parts of the world have different climates. Climate really affects the way people live. The food that grows, the houses that are built, the jobs, and even the types of things people do from day to day are all affected by climate.

☼ Find out more about some of the different climate zones on our planet.

Tropical Climates

1. Describe the weather in this climate zone: _____

_____

2. Name some areas that have a tropical climate: _____

_____

3. What type of foods do people in the tropics eat? _____

4. What types of homes do people live in? _____

Temperate Climate

1. Describe the weather in this climate zone: _____

_____

2. Name an area that has a temperate climate: _____

_____

3. What type of foods do people in this climate grow and eat? _____

4. What types of homes do people live in? _____

Desert Climate

1. Describe the weather in this climate zone: _____

_____

2. Name some areas that have a desert climate: _____

_____

3. What types of foods do people in this climate grow and eat? _____

4. What types of homes do people live in? _____

Name _____

Happy New Year!

☼ Use your library and other resources to learn more about how people around the world celebrate the New Year.

1. How do you and your family celebrate New Year's eve and day?

    _____

    _____

    _____

    _____

2. What are some well-known traditions and events for celebrating the New Year in the United States?

    _____

    _____

    _____

3. How do children in Belgium celebrate the New Year?

    _____

    _____

4. How do people in Japan celebrate the New Year?

    _____

    _____

5. How do people in Columbia get rid of all of the bad things from the year before? _____

    _____

6. When and how do people in Thailand celebrate the New Year?

    _____

    _____

7. When and how is the Chinese New Year celebrated?

    _____

    _____

Name_____

G'day Mate!

☼ Although Australians speak English, they say some things very differently than Americans. Look at the glossary of Australian words below. Then, use at least eight of the sayings in a short story about a trip to Australia.

Australian Glossary:

g'day—good day, hello

Oz—Australia

mate—a friend

tucker—food

biscuits (bikkie)—cookies

ta—thank you

fair dinkum—the truth, true

barbie—a barbecue

lolly water—soft drinks

boomer—a big kangaroo

joey—baby kangaroo

beaut—great or beauty

jumper—sweater

joggers—running shoes

petrol station—gas station

cool drink—soda pop

sussed—figured out

arvo—afternoon

How ya goin?—How are you?

tea—a drink or dinner

brekky—breakfast

snaggers—sausages

sangers—sandwich

How Countries are Governed

Content Area(s):

- reading and comprehension
- social studies
- research

Objectives:

In this section students:

- identify, locate, and use resource materials to find required information.
- research different types of government.
- interview people in the school or community.
- write a letter to an unknown pen pal in a foreign country.

Materials Required:

- library, computer, or other resource materials
- pencil or pen

Time:

- Approximately 30 minutes per lesson. These lessons might also be used as part of ongoing research.

Teaching Tips and Suggestions:

Wave That Flag (page 39)

- Talk about the resources students can use to find the country flags and how they might follow up to find out about the symbolism and meaning of the flags.

Governments (page 40)

- Establish different types of government in the class for a week or two at a time. Have groups of students be in charge of researching and establishing each government system. (Except a tyranny or dictatorship, those could be yours!)

Multicultural Communities (page 41)

- Make sure students understand the vocabulary. Share research reports in the class or have guest speakers give presentations.

Pen Pal (page 42)

- There are three Web sites that will help you find pen/key pals for your students:

    Web66 at **http://web66.coled.umn.edu/schools.html**

    IECC at **http://www.iecc.org**

    E-Pals at **http://www.epals.com**

    You can also search *Yahooligans* to locate this information.

Name_____

Wave That Flag

☺ Use your library or other resources to find the information to complete this activity page.

Each country of the world has its own flag, and each flag has meaning for the people of that country. Did you know that every part of the United States' flag has some meaning? The 50 stars represent the 50 states. There are 13 stripes to represent the original 13 colonies. The colors also have meaning: red is for hardiness and courage, white for purity and innocence, and blue for vigilance, perseverance, and justice.

☺ Find out which country each of the flags below comes from. Correctly color the flags and find out any special meanings associated with the flags.

1. Country:_____

   Special meanings: _____

   _____

   _____

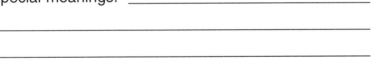

2. Country:_____

   Special meanings: _____

   _____

   _____

3. Country:_____

   Special meanings: _____

   _____

   _____

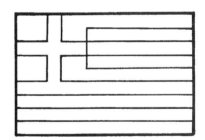

Challenge: Research what psychologists say about how colors make people feel. Record what you find on the back of this page. What colors do you find most often in flags of the world? Why do you think they are the most popular for flags?

Name _____

Governments

⚙ Use your library or other resources to find out more about world governments.

The government of a country is part of culture because it is part of the day-to-day life of a group of people. Research to find out more about different types of governments. For each type of government listed below, briefly explain how it works and then list at least three countries that have that type of government today.

Monarchy: _____
_____
_____
_____
Countries with Monarchies: _____

Republic: _____
_____
_____
_____
Countries that are Republics: _____

Communism: _____
_____
_____
_____
Communist Countries: _____

Parliamentary Government: _____
_____
_____
_____
Countries that have Parliaments: _____

Challenge: From what you have read, which do you think is the best form of government? On the back of this paper, explain your answer.

Name_____

Multicultural Communities

People from all over the world live in the United States. This means that people from many different cultural backgrounds live in the same communities. Talk to the people in your classroom, school, or community to learn more about the cultures that are part of your city or town.

○ Does anyone in your class, school, or community come from a different country? List the countries here: _____

_____

○ Find a person to interview who has a different culture than you.

1. What foods do they eat? _____

_____

2. What holidays do they celebrate? _____

_____

3. How do they celebrate special days? _____

_____

_____

_____

4. What languages do they speak? _____

_____

5. Why did they come to the United States? _____

_____

6. How are things in the United States different from the country they came from?

_____

_____

Challenge: Except for Native Americans, everyone who lives in the United States now came from a different country at some point. Research to find out what country or countries your ancestors came from.

Name _____

Pen Pal

Choose a country you would like to learn more about. Write a letter to a boy or girl who is your age in that country. Talk about your life and culture and ask questions to learn more about his or her life and culture. Be sure to include details about the land, climate, government, food, language, school, clothes, music, TV, sports, and anything else that is part of your life, or you would like to learn about his or her life.

Dear _____,

_____

_____

_____

_____

_____

_____

_____

_____

Your friend,

_____

Challenge: Now, talk to your teacher or parents about how to contact a pen/key pal in your chosen country. If you need to translate your letter into a different language, the Alta Vista Translation Site at **http://world.altavista.com** can help you.

Thinking about your Travels

Content Area(s):

- reading and comprehension
- social studies
- research

Objectives:

In this section students:

- identify, locate, and use resource materials to find required information.
- create a travel brochure promoting a visit to a foreign country.
- make a plan for traveling to a foreign country.
- reflect on thinking and learning experiences through the unit.

Materials Required:

- library, computer, or other resource materials
- pencil or pen

Time:

- Approximately 30 minutes per lesson. These lessons might also be used as part of ongoing research.

Teaching Tips and Suggestions:

Travel Brochure (page 44)

- Bring in some brochures for students to look at. Talk about the language used to make each place sound very attractive.
- Have a lesson or review on adjectives and require students to use a certain number of adjectives in their brochures.

Bon Voyage! (page 45)

- You might also include some lessons on how to organize and purchase an airline ticket, how to exchange money and the value of different currencies, or what vaccinations do.

Reflection Page (page 46)

- Allow students to talk in small groups to practice articulating their thoughts before they do the reflection page. This is a great assessment tool.

Name _____

Travel Brochure

✪ Use your library and other resources to research a country of your choice and develop a travel brochure. Use the outline below to help you.

(Catchy title) _____

_____

(Interesting introduction)_____

_____

_____

_____

(Country location) _____

_____

_____

_____

(Land and climate) _____

_____

_____

_____

(Best time of year to visit and why)

_____

_____

_____

_____

(Plants and wildlife) _____

_____

_____

_____

_____

(Draw or paste a picture of the country here.)

(History of the country) _____

_____

_____

_____

(The people, food, and culture)

_____

_____

_____

_____

(Things to do or see) _____

_____

_____

_____

_____

Name_____

Bon Voyage!

It is important to research foreign countries before you visit them. Some countries have different customs. Others have sicknesses that you may need to be vaccinated for. You also need to practice the language and decide when and what you want to visit on your trip.

⚙ Choose a country you would like to visit and use your library or other resources to complete the activities below to learn more about the country and prepare for your trip.

Destination: _____ Languages spoken there: _____

How will you get there? _____

What will the weather be like while you are there? _____

How will you travel around when you are there? _____

Where will you stay while you are there? _____

What types of food will you eat? _____

What is their money called? _____

How much money will you need? _____

Do you need to watch out for any dangers while you are there? _____

Will you need to get any shots (vaccinations) before you go?_____

What customs do you need to know about? _____

_____

What will you do while you are there? What special places will you visit?

_____

_____

_____

What will you pack? _____

_____

Challenge: Think of five things you will need to know how to ask or say when you visit your country. Write them on the back of this paper and translate them into the language spoken in the country you will be visiting using **http://world.altavista.com.**

Name _____

Reflection Page

☼ It is very important to reflect on how you think and how you learn. Think about what you have learned about world cultures and complete this page to share with a classmate and your teacher.

1. List at least five things you have learned while studying different cultures of the world:

   • _____

   • _____

   • _____

   • _____

   • _____

2. Which country would you most like to visit and why? _____

   _____

3. How has television, radio, the Internet, and other technology changed world cultures?

   _____

   _____

4. What are some reasons why we study other cultures of the world?

   _____

   _____

   _____

   _____

5. How does studying other countries help you learn more about the United States?

   _____

   _____

   _____

6. After studying world cultures, what do you better understand about your country and the world? _____

   _____

   _____

   _____

Answer Key

Page 7—Earth's Greatest Features

1. Asia; 2. Pacific Ocean, Atlantic Ocean, Indian Ocean, Arctic Ocean, South China Sea; 3. Everest and K2; 4. Nile-Africa, Amazon-South America, Yangtze-China; 5. Kilauea and Mauna Loa; 6. Norway; 7. Russia; 8. Mt. McKinley (or Denali)

Page 8—Languages Around the World

1. French: Quel est votre nom? Italian: Che cosa è il vostro nome?; 2. Italian: Dove vivete? Portuguese: Onde você vive?; 3. Spanish: Usted habla inglés? German: Sprechen Sie Englisch?; 4. Spanish: Estoy utilizando el Internet. German: Ich benutze das Internet.

Page 9—National Flags

Use the Web site to check student drawings.

Page 11—Festivals and Traditions

Answers will vary.

Page 12—Christmas Around the World

Answers will vary depending on the country the student chooses.

"Merry Christmas and a Happy New Year" in French: Joyeux Noel et Bonne Année; Spanish: Feliz Navidad y Prospero ano nuevo; Irish (Gaelic): Nollaig Shona duit; Japanese: Meri Kurisumasu soshite Akemashite Omedeto

Page 14—World Tour

1. 17,000 islands; 2. 3,200, equator; 3. Malaysia, Papua New Guinea, Singapore, Thailand, Vietnam, The Philippines, and Australia; 4. 179 million people; 5. rice; 6. Indian, Chinese, French, Creole, and English; 7. East of Madagascar; 8. "You gather that Mauritius was made first, and then heaven, and that heaven was copied after Mauritius"; 9. Answers will vary.

Page 15—Travel to Brazil

1. fifth; 2. 157 million people; 3. Portuguese; 4. Samba; 5. coffee; 6. Amazon; 7. pineapple, fig, mango, orange, and bignonia; 8. butterflies; 9. hydroelectric power plants; 10. second

Page 16—Journey to Japan

1. Hokkaido, Honshu, Kyushu, and Shikoku; 2. 126 million people; 3. rice, vegetables, fish, seaweed, sushi, and soba; 4. check student flags; 5. the red rising sun; 6. Japan specializes in cars and electronics such as stereos, video games, and televisions. They are also leaders in computer technology; 7. check student drawings; 8. The Tale of Genji; 9. Sumimasen means "excuse me," Arigato means "thank you," and Konnichi wa means "good morning."

Page 17—A Visit to Ireland

1. About 3.5 million people; 2. Much of the soil in Ireland is bog-like and trees cannot grow. Grass does just fine and looks much greener than trees; 3. English and Irish (Gaelic); 4. stewed tomatoes and spuds (potatoes); 5. Dublin; 6. Eire; 7. St Patrick's Day on March 17th; 8. Answers will vary.

Page 18—The Gift of the Nile

1. Northeastern Africa; 2. around 51,000 years ago; 3. governments, writing, and mathematics; 4. Islam; 5. Galabayya; 6. The Sahara Desert; 7. If the Nile was not there, then people would not be able to survive in the Sahara Desert; 8. 99%; 9. Felahin; 10. A town in central Egypt that people visit to see the ruins of great temples; 11. Hieroglyphics; 12. 66 feet, 240 feet; 13. trains, buses, and automobiles; 14. camels; 15. Red Sea and Mediterranean Sea

Page 20—The Island Continent

1. It is the only continent that is comprised of a single country and it is completely surrounded by water; 2. the Outback; 3. summer; 4. a mammal that has its young early and then continues the development in a pocket or pouch; 5. When European explorers asked a native Australian what the strange, hopping animal was called, he replied, "Kangaroo," which means, "I do not understand."; 6. Kookaburra; 7. Aborigines; 8. over 40,000 years ago; 9. Answers will vary; 10. Cricket and Australian-Rules Football

Page 21—The United Kingdom

1. check student maps; 2. The United Kingdom of Great Britain and Northern Ireland; 3. the United Kingdom, the UK, Great Britain, and Britain; 4. false; 5. false; 6. true; 7. false; 8. The British used to rule over one forth of the world's people; 9. roast beef and Yorkshire pudding; 10. Answers will vary; 11. Wimbledon Tennis Championship; 12. golf; 13. the pound; 14. The Union Jack

Page 23—Land of Ice and Fire

1. Glaciers are next to hot springs, geysers, and volcanoes; 2. natural hot water running through pipes in the floor or walls of their homes; 3. 800s, Vikings; 4. Answers will vary; 5. Answers will vary; 6. lamb; 7. Shark that has been rotting underground for four months, ram's testicles, and boiled sheep's head; 8. Reykjavik; 9. She was the world's first female head of state.

Answer Key *(cont.)*

Page 24—The Largest Country

1. Europe and Asia; 2. Northeastern Siberia; 3. 10%; 4. 800s–1922: Czars and empresses ruled over all aspects of life. 1922–1991: The Soviet Union was the most powerful communist country in the world. 1991–present: They have a new constitution, have elected a president, and have more freedoms; 5. There are housing shortages due to so many buildings being destroyed during WWI; 6. Answers will vary; 7. museum or ballet; 8. Sturgeon eggs; 9. hike and pick mushrooms

Page 26—The Kingdom of Nepal

1. the Himalaya, the Hills and Valleys, and the Terai; 2. They are the tallest mountains on the planet; 3. corn, jute, millet, mustard, rice, sugar cane, and tobacco; 4. Kathmandu Valley; 5. Sherpas are Himalayan guides and mountain climbers; 6. Gurkhas are Nepalese soldiers in the British Army; 7. Hindu; 8. Do: take off shoes, ask permission before taking photos; Don't: go if you are not allowed, wear any leather, touch offerings or people, eat beef or kill female animals; 9. They have more festivals than there are days in the year.

Page 27—Saudi Arabia

1. petroleum; 2. Rub Khali; 3. It was joined together by the Saud family and is on the Arabian Peninsula; 4. Answers will vary; 5. There are rules about how to dress, eat, play, speak, and live; 7. Boys/Men: basketball, volleyball, swimming, wrestling, roller skating, soccer; Girls/Women: volleyball (girls only), visiting each other, family outings, volunteer work

Page 28—Land of Smiles

1. February to May = hot, June to October = rainy, November to January = cool; 2. Land is being taken for farming and poachers are killing animals for money; 3. Siam; 4. 96%; 5. They have shaved heads and wear orange robes; 6. A greeting where people put their palms together and bow; 7. check student drawings; 8. Answers will vary; 9. hacky sack

Page 30—¡Holá Amigos!

1. The northern part of the country is very dry with deserts and cactus while the southern part is more tropical and has jungles; 2. a Mestizo; 3. corn; 4. Answers will vary; 5. sombrero, serape, huaraches; 6. Answers will vary.

Page 31—Greece

1. The countries that were settled or influenced by Romans or Europeans; 2. Athens; 3. Ancient Greek stories that used gods and goddesses to explain the known and unknown world; 4. Mt. Olympus; 5. The God of the sky and ruler of all other gods; 6. Answers will vary; 7. The Olympics; 8. talk, play games, soccer, basketball, do track and field sports, visit friends, meet family; 9. 9:00 P.M.; 10. A taverna; 11. Answers will vary

Page 32—Jambo!

1. The highlands of the southwest because there is enough rain for farming; 2. journey; 3. 1963; 4. Answers will vary; 5. carve statues, make jewelry, create dances; 6. corn; 7. running; 8. Jamhuri ya Kenya; 9. Swahili; 10. Kenya shilling

Pages 34–35—General Activity Pages

Answers will vary.

Page 36—Happy New Year

1–2. Answers will vary; Following are some examples of how the New Year is celebrated. 3. Children light fireworks and then spend a few days visiting relatives; 4. The famous temples ring 108 bells at midnight. In the morning the people drink spiced Japanese sake; 5. They burn "Mr. Old Year." They make a big stuffed doll that represents the old year and stuff if with mementos of their bad memories. Then they burn the doll to get rid of the bad feelings; 6. The Thai New Year is celebrated on April 13, or "Song-Klarn Day." Thai people often go back to their hometowns to visit their elders; 7. The date is determined by the Chinese calendar. It is a time to repay debts, enjoy feasts, give to friends and relatives, and remember ancestors.

Pages 37—39—General Activity Pages

Answers will vary.

Page 40—Governments

Monarchy: an autocracy governed by a leader who usually inherits the authority and rules for life; Republic: a country governed by the people or their elected representatives; Communism: a form of government that abolishes private ownership; Parliament: an assembly that has supreme legislative powers. Definitions from http://www.dictionary.com/.

Page 41–46—General Activity Pages

Answers will vary.